The Last Days of John Brown

THE LAST DAYS OF JOHN BROWN

HENRY DAVID THOREAU

COSIMOCLASSICS
NEW YORK

John Brown's Speech to the Court at his Trial," originally a speech delivered to the court before which Brown was tried at Charlestown, West Virginia, November 2, 1859; "Remarks After the Hanging of John Brown," originally a lecture read on December 2, 1859; "The Last Days of John Brown," originally a lecture read at North Elba, on July 4, 1860
This edition published by Cosimo Classics in 2021

Cover copyright © 2021 by Cosimo, Inc.
Cover image, mural of "The Tragic Prelude of John Brown," by John Stewart Curry, 1938. Sourced from Wikimedia Commons, *https://commons.wikimedia.org/wiki/File:The_Tragic_Prelude_John_Brown.jpg*
Cover design by www.heatherkern.com
Interior design by Jeannine H. Ford

ISBN: 978-1-64679-489-8

This edition is a replica of a rare classic. As such, it is possible that some of the text might be blurred or of reduced print quality. Thank you for your understanding, and we wish you a pleasant reading experience.

> Cosimo aims to publish books that inspire, inform, and engage readers worldwide. We use innovative print-on-demand technology that enables books to be printed based on specific customer needs. This approach eliminates an artificial scarcity of publications and allows us to distribute books in the most efficient and environmentally sustainable manner. Cosimo also works with printers and paper manufacturers who practice and encourage sustainable forest management, using paper that has been certified by the FSC, SFI, and PEFC whenever possible.

Ordering Information:
Cosimo publications are available at online bookstores. They may also be purchased for educational, business, or promotional use:
Bulk orders: Special discounts are available on bulk orders for reading groups, organizations, businesses, and others.
Custom-label orders: We offer selected books with your customized cover or logo of choice.

For more information, contact us at www.cosimobooks.com.

The Last Days of John Brown

TABLE OF CONTENTS

John Brown's Address to the Court at his Trial
by John Brown
–9–

Remarks After the Hanging of John Brown
by Henry David Thoreau
–12–

The Last Days of John Brown
by Henry David Thoreau
–17–

JOHN BROWN'S ADDRESS TO THE COURT AT HIS TRIAL

Address of John Brown to the Virginia Court at Charles Town, Virginia on November 2, 1859. Mr. Brown, upon inquiry whether he had anything to say why sentences should not be pronounced upon him, in a clear, distinct voice, replied:

I have, may it please the court, a few words to say. In the first place, I deny everything but what I have all along admitted,—the design on my part to free slaves. I intended certainly to have made a clean thing of that matter, as I did last winter, when I went into Missouri and took slaves without the snapping of a gun on either side, moved them through the country, and finally left them in Canada. I designed to do the same thing again, on a larger scale. That was all I intended. I never did intend murder, or treason, or the destruction of property, or to excite or incite slaves to rebellion, or to make insurrection.

I have another objection; and that is, it is unjust that I should suffer such a penalty. Had I interfered in the manner which I admit, and which I admit has been fairly proved (for I admire the truthfulness and candor of the greater portion of the witnesses who have testified in this case),—had I so interfered in behalf of the rich, the powerful, the intelligent, the so-called great, or in behalf of any of their friends—either father, mother, sister, wife, or children, or any of that class—and suffered and sacrificed what I have in this interference, it would have been all right; and every man in this court would have deemed it an act worthy of reward rather than punishment.

The court acknowledges, as I suppose, the validity of the law of God. I see a book kissed here which I suppose to be the Bible, or at least the New Testament. That teaches me that all things whatsoever I would that men should do to me, I should do even so to them. It teaches me further to "remember them that are in bonds, as bound with them." I endeavored to act up to that instruction. I say, I am too young to understand that God is any respecter of persons. I believe that to have interfered as I have done—as I have always freely admitted I have done—in behalf of His despied poor, was not wrong, but right. Now if it is deemed necessary that I should forfeit my life for the furtherance of the ends of justice, and mingle my blood further with the blood of my children and with the blood of millions in this slave country whose rights are disregarded by wicked, cruel, and unjust enactments.—I submit; so let it be done!

Let me say one word further: I feel entirely satisfied with the treatment I have received on my trial. Considering all the circumstances, it has been more generous than I expected. I feel no consciousness of my guilt. I have stated from the first what was my intention, and what was not. I never had any design against the life of any person, nor any disposition to commit treason, or excite slaves to rebel, or make any general insurrection. I never encouraged any man to do so, but always discouraged any idea of any kind.

Let me say also, a word in regard to the statements made by some to those connected with me. I hear it has been said by some of them that I have induced them to join me. But the contrary is true. I do not say this to injure them, but as regretting their weakness. There is not one of them but joined me of his own accord, and the greater part of them at their own expense. A number of them I never saw, and never had a word of conversation with, till the day they came to me; and that was for the purpose I have stated.

Now I have done.

REMARKS AFTER THE HANGING OF JOHN BROWN

At the services held in Concord, Massachusetts, December 2, 1859, in commemoration of John Brown, executed that day, Mr. Henry David Thoreau said:

So universal and widely related is any transcendent moral greatness, and so nearly identical with greatness every where and in every age, — as a pyramid contracts the nearer you approach its apex, — that, when I now look over my commonplace book of poetry, I find that the best of it is oftenest applicable, in part or wholly, to the case of Captain Brown. Only what is true, and strong, and solemnly earnest, will recommend itself to our mood at this time. Almost any noble verse may be read, either as his elegy or eulogy, or be made the text of an oration on him. Indeed, such are now discovered to be the parts of a universal liturgy, applicable to those rare cases of heroes and martyrs, for which the ritual of no church has provided. This is the formula established on high — their burial service — to which every great genius has contributed its stanza or line. As Marvell wrote:

> "When the sword glitters o'er the judge's head,
> And fear has coward churchmen silenced,
> Then is the poet's time; 't is then he draws,
> And single fights forsaken virtue's cause;
> He, when the wheel of empire whirleth back,
> And though the world's disjointed axle crack,
> Sings still of ancient rights and better times,
> Seeks suffering good, arraigns successful crimes."

The sense of grand poetry, read by the light of this event, is brought out distinctly, like an invisible writing held to the fire:

> All heads must come
> To the cold tomb,—
> Only the actions of the just
> Smell sweet and blossom in the dust.

We have heard that the Boston lady who recently visited our hero in prison found him wearing still the clothes, all cut and torn by sabres and by bayonet thrusts, in which he had been taken prisoner; and thus he had gone to his trial, and without a hat. She spent her time in prison mending those clothes, and, for a memento, brought home a pin covered with blood.

> What are the clothes that endure?
> "The, garments lasting evermore
> Are works of mercy to the poor;
> And neither tetter, time, nor moth
> Shall fray that silk or fret this cloth."

The well-known verses called "The Soul's Errand," supposed, by some, to have been written by Sir Walter Raleigh, when he was expecting to be executed the following day, are at least worthy of such an origin, and are equally applicable to the present case. Hear them:

THE SOUL'S ERRAND.

Go, soul, the body's guest,
Upon a thankless arrant;
Fear not to touch the best;
The truth shall be thy warrant:
Go, since I needs must die,
And give the world the lie.

Go, tell the Court it glows
And shines like rotten wood;
Go, tell the church it shows
What's good, and doth no good;
If church and court reply,
Then give them both the lie.

Tell potentates they live
Acting by others' actions;
Not loved unless they give,
Not strong but by their factions:
If potentates reply,
Give potentates the lie.

Tell men of high condition,
That rule affairs of state,
Their purpose is ambition,
Their practice only hate;
And if they once reply,
Then give them all the lie.

Tell Zeal, it lacks devotion;
Tell Love, it is but lust;
Tell Time, it is but motion;

Tell Flesh, it is but dust;
And wish them not reply,
For thou must give the lie.
Tell Age, it daily wasteth;
Tell Honor, how it alters;
Tell Beauty, how she blasteth;

Tell Favor, how she falters;
And, as they shall reply,
Give each of them the lie.

Tell Fortune of her blindness;
Tell Nature of decay;
Tell Friendship of unkindness;
Tell Justice of delay;
And if they dare reply,
Then give them all the lie.
And when thou hast, as I
Commanded thee, done blabbing,
Although to give the lie
Deserves no less than stabbing,
Yet, stab at thee who will,
No stab the soul can kill.

"When I am dead,
Let not the day be writ,"
Nor bell be tolled
"Love will remember it"
When hate is cold.

Thoreau also read a number of poetical passages, selected for the occasion by another citizen of Concord:

> *How sleep the Brave* by William Collins
> excerpts from *The Death of Wallenstein* by Frederich Schiller (translated by Samuel Taylor Coleridge)
> excerpts from *Alas! What boots the long laborious quest* by William Wordsworth
> excerpts from *Maud* by Alfred Tennyson
> excerpts from *Conspiracy of Charles, Duke of Byron* by George Chapman
> *The Character of a Happy Life* by Henry Wotton

Thoreau then read his own translation of Tacitus:

You, Agricola, are fortunate, not only because your life was glorious, but because your death was timely. As they tell us who heard your last words, unchanged and willing you accepted your fate; as if, as far as in your power, you would make the emperor appear innocent. But, besides the bitterness of having lost a parent, it adds to our grief, that it was not permitted us to minister to your health, ... to gaze on your countenance, and receive your last embrace; surely, we might have caught some words and commands which we could have treasured in the inmost part of our souls. This is our pain, this our wound... You were buried with the fewer tears, and in your last earthly light, your eyes looked around for something which they did not see.

If there is any abode for the spirits of the pious; if, as wise men suppose, great souls are not extinguished with the body, may you rest placidly, and call your family from weak regrets, and womanly laments, to the contemplation of your virtues, which must not be lamented, either silently or aloud. Let us honor you by our admiration, rather than by short-lived praises, and, if nature aid us, by our emulation of you. That is true honor, that the piety of whoever is most akin to you. This also I would teach your family, so to venerate your memory, as to call to mind all your actions and words, and embrace your character and the form of your soul, rather than of your body; not because I think that statues which are made of marble or brass are to be condemned, but as the features of men, so images of the features, are frail and perishable. The form of the soul is eternal; and this we can retain and express, not by a foreign material and art, but by our own lives. Whatever of Agricola we have loved, whatever we have admired, remains, and will remain, in the minds of men, and the records of history, through the eternity of ages. For oblivion will overtake many of the ancients, as if they were inglorious and ignoble: Agricola, described and transmitted to posterity, will survive.

THE LAST DAYS OF JOHN BROWN

Read by
Mr. Henry David Thoreau at North Elba, July 4, 1860.

John Brown's career for the last six weeks of his life was meteor-like, flashing through the darkness in which we live. I know of nothing so miraculous in our history.

If any person, in a lecture or conversation at that time, cited any ancient example of heroism, such as Cato or Tell or Winkelried, passing over the recent deeds and words of Brown, it was felt by any intelligent audience of Northern men to be tame and inexcusably farfetched.

For my own part, I commonly attend more to nature than to man, but any affecting human event may blind our eyes to natural objects. I was so absorbed in him as to be surprised whenever I detected the routine of the natural world surviving still, or met persons going about their affairs indifferent. It appeared strange to me that the "little dipper" should be still diving quietly in the river, as of yore; and it suggested that this bird might continue to dive here when Concord should be no more.

I felt that he, a prisoner in the midst of his enemies, and under sentence of death, if consulted as to his next step or resource, could answer more wisely than all his countrymen beside. He best understood his position; he contemplated it most calmly. Comparatively, all other men, North and South, were beside themselves. Our thoughts could not revert to any greater or wiser or better man with whom to contrast him, for he, then and there, was above them all. The man this country was about to hang appeared the greatest and best in it.

Years were not required for a revolution of public opinion; days, nay hours, produced marked changes in this case. Fifty who were ready to say on going into our meeting in honor of him in Concord, that he ought to be hung, would not say it when they came out. They heard his words read; they saw the earnest faces of the congregation; and perhaps they joined at last in singing the hymn in his praise.

The order of instructors was reversed. I heard that one preacher, who at first was shocked and stood aloof, felt obliged at last, after he was hung, to make him the subject of a sermon, in which, to some extent, he eulogized the man, but said that his act was a failure. An influential class-teacher thought it necessary, after the services, to tell his grown-up pupils, that at first he thought as the preacher did then, but now he thought that John Brown was right. But it was understood that his pupils were as much ahead of the teacher as he was ahead of the priest; and I know for a certainty, that very little boys at home had already asked their parents, in a tone of surprise, why God did not interfere to save him. In each case, the constituted teachers were only half conscious that they were not leading, but being dragged, with some loss of time and power.

The more conscientious preachers, the Bible men, they who talk about principle, and doing to others as you would that they should do unto you,—how could they fail to recognize him, by far the greatest preacher of them all, with the Bible in his life and in his acts, the embodiment of principle, who actually carried out the golden rule? All whose moral sense had been aroused, who had a calling from on high to preach, sided with him. What confessions he extracted from the cold and conservative! It is remarkable, but on the whole it is well, that it did not prove the occasion for a new sect of Brownites being formed in our midst.

They, whether within the Church or out of it, who adhere to the spirit and let go the letter, and are accordingly called infidel, were as usual foremost to recognize him. Men have been hung in the South before for attempting to rescue slaves, and the North was not much stirred by it. Whence, then, this wonderful difference? We were not so sure of their devotion to principle. We made a subtle distinction, forgot human laws, and did homage to an idea. The North, I mean the living North, was suddenly all transcendental. It went behind the human law, it went behind the apparent failure, and recognized eternal justice and glory. Commonly, men live according to a formula, and are satisfied if the order of law is observed, but in this instance they, to some extent, returned to original perceptions, and there was a slight revival of old religion. They saw that what was called order was confusion, what was called justice, injustice, and that the best was deemed the worst. This attitude suggested a more intelligent and generous spirit than that which actuated our forefathers, and the possibility, in the course of ages, of a revolution in behalf of another and an oppressed people.

Most Northern men, and a few Southern ones, were wonderfully stirred by Brown's behavior and words. They saw and felt that they were heroic and noble, and that there had been nothing quite equal to them in their kind in this country, or in the recent history of the world. But the minority were unmoved by them. They were only surprised and provoked by the attitude of their neighbors. They saw that Brown was brave, and that he believed that he had done right, but they did not detect any further peculiarity in him. Not being accustomed to make fine distinctions, or to appreciate magnanimity, they read his letters and speeches as if they read them not. They were not aware when they approached a heroic statement,—they did not know when they burned. They did not feel that he spoke with authority, and hence they only remembered that the law must be executed. They remembered the old formula, but did not hear the new revelation. The man who does not recognize in Brown's words a wisdom and nobleness, and therefore an authority, superior to our laws, is a modern Democrat. This is the test by which to discover him. He is not wilfully but constitutionally blind on this side, and he is consistent with himself. Such has been his past life; no doubt of it. In like manner he has read history and his Bible, and he accepts, or seems to accept, the last only as an established formula, and not because he has been convicted by it. You will not find kindred sentiments in his commonplace book, if he has one.

When a noble deed is done, who is likely to appreciate it? They who are noble themselves. I was not surprised that certain of my neighbors spoke of John Brown as an ordinary felon, for who are they? They have either much flesh, or much office, or much coarseness of some kind. They are not ethereal natures in any sense. The dark qualities predominate in them. Several of them are decidedly pachydermatous. I say it in sorrow, not in anger. How can a man behold the light, who has no answering inward light? They are true to their right, but when they look this way they see nothing, they are blind. For the children of the light to contend with them is as if there should be a contest between eagles and owls. Show me a man who feels bitterly toward John Brown, and let me hear what noble verse he can repeat. He'll be as dumb as if his lips were stone.

It is not every man who can be a Christian, even in a very moderate sense, whatever education you give him. It is a matter of constitution and temperament, after all. He may have to be born again many times. I have known many a man who pretended to be a Christian, in whom it was ridiculous, for he had no genius for it. It is not every man who can be a freeman, even.

Editors persevered for a good while in saying that Brown was crazy; but at last they said only that it was "a crazy scheme," and the only evidence brought to prove it was that it cost him his life. I have no doubt that if he had gone with five thousand men, liberated a thousand slaves, killed a hundred or two slaveholders, and had as many more killed on his own side, but not lost his own life, these same editors would have called it by a more respectable name. Yet he has been far more successful than that. He has liberated many thousands of slaves, both North and South. They seem to have known nothing about living or dying for a principle. They all called him crazy then; who calls him crazy now?

All through the excitement occasioned by his remarkable attempt and subsequent behavior, the Massachusetts Legislature, not taking any steps for the defence of her citizens who were likely to be carried to Virginia as witnesses and exposed to the violence of a slaveholding mob, was wholly absorbed in a liquor-agency question, and indulging in poor jokes on the word "extension." Bad spirits occupied their thoughts. I am sure that no statesman up to the occasion could have attended to that question at all at that time,—a very vulgar question to attend to at any time!

When I looked into a liturgy of the Church of England, printed near the end of the last century, in order to find a service applicable to the case of Brown, I found that the only martyr recognized and provided for by it was King Charles the First, an eminent scamp. Of all the inhabitants of England and of the world, he was the only one, according to this authority, whom that church had made a martyr and saint of; and for more than a century it had celebrated his martyrdom, so called, by an annual service. What a satire on the Church is that!

Look not to legislatures and churches for your guidance, nor to any soulless incorporated bodies, but to inspirited or inspired ones. What avail all your scholarly accomplishments and learning, compared with wisdom and manhood? To omit his other behavior, see what a work this comparatively unread and unlettered man wrote within six weeks. Where is our professor of belles-lettres or of logic and rhetoric, who can write so well? He wrote in prison, not a History of the World, like Raleigh, but an American book which I think will live longer than that. I do not know of such words, uttered under such circumstances, and so copiously withal, in Roman or English or any history. What a variety of themes he touched on in that short space! There are words in that letter to his wife, respecting the education of his daughters, which deserve to be framed and hung over every mantelpiece in the land. Compare this earnest wisdom with that of Poor Richard.

The death of Irving, which at any other time would have attracted universal attention, having occurred while these things were transpiring, went almost unobserved. I shall have to read of it in the biography of authors.

Literary gentlemen, editors, and critics, think that they know how to write, because they have studied grammar and rhetoric; but they are egregiously mistaken.

The art of composition is as simple as the discharge of a bullet from a rifle, and its masterpieces imply an infinitely greater force behind them. This unlettered man's speaking and writing are standard English. Some words and phrases deemed vulgarisms and Americanisms before, he has made standard American; such as "It will pay" It suggests that the one great rule of composition,—and if I were a professor of rhetoric I should insist on this,—is, to speak the truth. This first, this second, this third; pebbles in your mouth or not. This demands earnestness and manhood chiefly.

We seem to have forgotten that the expression, a liberal education, originally meant among the Romans one worthy of free men; while the learning of trades and professions by which to get your livelihood merely was considered worthy of slaves only. But taking a hint from the word, I would go a step farther, and say, that it is not the man of wealth and leisure simply, though devoted to art, or science, or literature, who, in a true sense, is liberally educated, but only the earnest and free man. In a slaveholding country like this, there can be no such thing as a liberal education tolerated by the State; and those scholars of Austria and France who, however learned they may be, are contented under their tyrannies, have received only a servile education.

Nothing could his enemies do, but it redounded to his infinite advantage,—that is, to the advantage of his cause. They did not hang him at once, but reserved him to preach to them. And then there was another great blunder. They did not hang his four followers with him; that scene was still postponed; and so his victory was prolonged and completed. No theatrical manager could have arranged things so wisely to give effect to his behavior and words. And who, think you, was the manager? Who placed the slave-woman and her child, whom he stooped to kiss for a symbol, between his prison and the gallows?

We soon saw, as he saw, that he was not to be pardoned or rescued by men. That would have been to disarm him, to restore to him a material weapon, a Sharpe's rifle, when he had taken up the sword of the spirit,—the sword with which he has really won his greatest and most memorable victories. Now he has not laid aside the sword of the spirit, for he is pure spirit himself, and his sword is pure spirit also.

> "He nothing common did or mean
> Upon that memorable scene,
> Nor called the gods with vulgar spite,
> To vindicate his helpless right;
> But bowed his comely head
> Down as upon a bed."

What a transit was that of his horizontal body alone, but just cut down from the gallows-tree! We read, that at such a time it passed through Philadelphia, and by Saturday night had reached New York. Thus, like a meteor it shot through the Union from the Southern regions toward the North! No such freight had the cars borne since they carried him Southward alive.

On the day of his translation, I heard, to be sure, that he was hung, but I did not know what that meant; I felt no sorrow on that account; but not for a day or two did I even hear that he was dead, and not after any number of days shall I believe it. Of all the men who were said to be my contemporaries, it seemed to me that John Brown was the only one who had not died. I never hear of a man named Brown now,—and I hear of them pretty often,—I never hear of any particularly brave and earnest man, but my first thought is of John Brown, and what relation he may be to him. I meet him at every turn. He is more alive than ever he was. He has earned immortality. He is not confined to North Elba nor to Kansas. He is no longer working in secret. He works in public, and in the clearest light that shines on this land.

COSIMO

COSIMO is a specialty publisher of books and publications that inspire, inform, and engage readers. Our mission is to offer unique books to niche audiences around the world.

COSIMO BOOKS publishes books and publications for innovative authors, nonprofit organizations, and businesses. **COSIMO BOOKS** specializes in bringing books back into print, publishing new books quickly and effectively, and making these publications available to readers around the world.

COSIMO CLASSICS offers a collection of distinctive titles by the great authors and thinkers throughout the ages. At **COSIMO CLASSICS** timeless works find new life as affordable books, covering a variety of subjects including: Business, Economics, History, Personal Development, Philosophy, Religion & Spirituality, and much more!

COSIMO REPORTS publishes public reports that affect your world, from global trends to the economy, and from health to geopolitics.

FOR MORE INFORMATION CONTACT US AT
INFO@COSIMOBOOKS.COM

- if you are a book lover interested in our current catalog of books

- if you represent a bookstore, book club, or anyone else interested in special discounts for bulk purchases

- if you are an author who wants to get published

- if you represent an organization or business seeking to publish books and other publications for your members, donors, or customers.

COSIMO BOOKS ARE ALWAYS AVAILABLE AT ONLINE BOOKSTORES

VISIT COSIMOBOOKS.COM
BE INSPIRED, BE INFORMED

CPSIA information can be obtained
at www.ICGtesting.com
Printed in the USA
LVHW041315310522
720087LV00003B/306